Original title:

Witty Words in the Wildwood

Copyright © 2025 Creative Arts Management OÜ
All rights reserved.

Author: Maya Livingston
ISBN HARDBACK: 978-1-80567-285-2
ISBN PAPERBACK: 978-1-80567-584-6

Mirthful Moments in Moss-Covered Groves

In the grove where giggles grow,
Squirrels chatter, putting on a show.
The flowers dance in a frolicsome breeze,
While bees buzz by with merry pleas.

A frog hops by with a jaunty croak,
Telling tales of a sleepy oak.
The sunlight winks through leaves so bright,
As mushrooms chuckle in pure delight.

A rabbit jests with a twitching nose,
Spreading rumors where laughter flows.
The old wise owl gives a knowing grin,
As chipmunks race for the latest din.

With each rustle and rustle, the woods unfold,
A tapestry woven of stories told.
In this verdant nook, joy intertwines,
Where nature's laughter is simply divine.

Fanciful Words in Ferny Nooks

In a glade where ferns do sway,

A rabbit tells jokes all day.

The squirrels clap, the owls grin wide,

As giggles echo through the tide.

The fox cracks wise with a sly wink,

While mushrooms chuckle, who'd ever think?

Each leaf a witness, each branch a friend,

Laughter resounds until the day's end.

The Chuckle of the Crow

A crow with a caper, perched on a limb,

Spouting tall tales with a theatrical whim.

He caws of a snail that outran the breeze,

Claiming it danced with the swaying trees.

Crickets all gather, their tunes in the air,

To listen and laugh at the crow's wild flair.

With every flap, he stirs up the fun,

Stories and giggles 'til the day is done.

Amusing Anecdotes Whispered by the Wind

The wind carries giggles from leaf to leaf,

Sharing tales that swap joy for grief.

It whispers of flowers that tickle their toes,

And how daisies wore hats, only the wind knows.

Through every nook, secrets collide,

With laughter and jests twirling like a tide.

Breezes conspire in merriment's wake,

As giggles abound in every quake.

Riddles Borne on Rustling Breezes

In the rustle of leaves, a riddle takes flight,

What has wings but cannot take height?

The breeze, it chuckles, then answers with glee,

A shadow that dances when you're hard to see.

A riddle for creatures both clever and fun,

In a world where laughter is never quite done.

So listen closely, the mysteries play,

In the rustling boughs, where giggles sway.

Eclectic Echoes of the Evergreen

Beneath the boughs, where squirrels play,
A bird sings jokes throughout the day.
The trees all chuckle, leaves in a dance,
As shadows prance in nature's trance.

A pinecone drops with a gentle plop,
While crickets laugh till their chirps just stop.
The brook joins in with a gurgled cheer,
It seems that humor lingers near.

Mirthful Musings of the Meadow

In fields of bright where daisies sprout,
A rabbit hops, never in doubt.
He tells the flowers, "Life's but a game!"
Each petal rolls, joining his claim.

The buzz of bees knows just the tune,
While butterflies dance beneath the moon.
With every leap, a giggle spreads,
As nature sings what laughter weds.

Banter on the Breezy Blow

The wind whispers secrets, soft and sly,
While leaves rustle, laughing as they fly.
A dandelion wishes with every puff,
Its dreams float free – oh, isn't that tough?

A fox approaching with a sly little grin,
He tips his hat; let the games begin!
The clouds above join in with their jest,
Fluffy and funny, they laugh at the rest.

Enigmatic Echoes from the Elms

Under the elms, where riddles bloom,
A gnome mumbles tales that spellbound the gloom.
He chuckles at shadows that flicker and fade,
In mystery's laughter, he cleverly played.

The owls pop in with a wink and a hoot,
Their wisdom wrapped snug in a comical suit.
Whispers of secrets float thick in the air,
Every glance exchanged holds a humorous flair.

Jostle of Joy in the Jungle Gym

Swinging high amidst the vines,
Laughter echoes, bright designs.
Monkeys dance in silly plight,
Chasing shadows, pure delight.

Slides that twist like tangled fate,
Where giggles flow and never wait.
Bouncing balls with squeaky cheer,
Joyful noise for all to hear.

Silly Secrets of the Sun-Dappled Path

Wandering where the sunlight plays,
Spinning tales of silly ways.
Butterflies with jests to share,
Twirl and frolic in the air.

Rustling leaves hold playful schemes,
Whispering of the silliest dreams.
Tickled by a breezy laugh,
Nature's joy, a crazy path.

Quirks of the Quiet Quagmire

In bogs where frogs don silly hats,
Lurking moose and talkative bats.
Sticky mud with cheeky grins,
Steps that squelch where laughter spins.

Marshy quirks in sticky plight,
Dance of critters, pure delight.
Splashing puddles, big and small,
Nature's giggles, heard by all.

Frolicsome Folklore of the Ferns

Ferns that giggle in the breeze,
Whisper tales among the trees.
Squirrels sporting nutty modes,
Chuckle with their acorn loads.

Dancing shadows, frolicking friends,
Where the laughter never ends.
Frolicsome fables bloom and grow,
In nature's laughter, joy will flow.

Satire in the Sunlit Glades

In glades where shadows lightly dance,
The trees tell jokes; they take a chance.
A squirrel trips, now what a sight,
He laughs and claims he'll fly tonight.

The owl hoots puns from high above,
While bees buzz by with misspelled love.
Each leaf's a line, each twig a quip,
In nature's play, we take a dip.

A deer in shades, now what a look,
He reads a tale from a storybook.
With every chuckle, they all cheer,
In sunlight's warmth, all jokes are clear.

So if you roam through vibrant scenes,
Just note the jokes hidden among the greens.
For nature's laughter's all around,
In every bush, in every sound.

Gags along the Gnarled Grasses

Amidst the gnarled and rustled base,
A rabbit grins, a silly face.
With every hop, a pun takes flight,
As daisies giggle, oh what a sight!

The grasses sway, a minstrel's tune,
While crickets chirp beneath the moon.
A hedgehog jokes about his spines,
A clever jest, oh how it shines!

In this green stage, the antics grow,
Where laughter seeds in every row.
An acorn drops, the jesters cheer,
And all the woods catch every ear.

So wander here, where fun abounds,
In every nook, a laugh resounds.
The wilds are rich with playful airs,
Come join the tune; the forest shares.

Frolicsome Fables from the Ferns

In ferns where whispers tickle low,
The tales unfold, they twist and flow.
A fox in boots has lost his way,
He asks the snail for tips today.

Each fable shared is steeped in cheer,
With laughter rising loud and clear.
A badger's joke about his style,
Will make you grin for quite a while.

In this green nook, they all convene,
Telling stories, both sweet and keen.
A toucan's laugh can rattle trees,
While frisky winds play tag with leaves.

So linger here, let giggles soar,
With nature's jesters, come explore.
For every fern, a riddle hides,
In playful shade, where joy abides.

Snickers Surrounded by Thickets

In thickets thick where shadows play,
A witty hare leads games all day.
With cheeky grins and tail held high,
It's pure delight; oh me, oh my!

The thorns are witnesses, so sly,
As squirrels trade jokes, oh how they fly.
Each rustle hints at humor's art,
In every snicker, warmth does start.

The pond reflects a chuckling frog,
As crickets join in sounds of smog.
A hedgehog rolls his eyes, says, 'Woe!'
With every quirk, the laughter grows.

Surrounded by thickets, wild and green,
Nature's jesters make quite a scene.
So if you wander, stop and see,
The snickers bloom like flowers free.

Whispers of Clever Canopies

In the shade where shadows play,
Laughter dances, bright and gay.
Squirrels chatter, puns in tow,
Acorns drop with a friendly hello.

Breezes carry cheeky jests,
Leaves giggle in nature's nests.
Branches sway with playful cheer,
Revealing secrets for all to hear.

Puns Beneath the Pines

Pinecones plop with a splat and a grin,
Whispering jokes that draw you in.
Funny faces of tree bark twist,
Inviting you to join the tryst.

Mice in tiny shoes can't help but dance,
As shadows waltz in a merry prance.
Underneath, giggles softly flow,
Nature's humor puts on a show.

Banter Amongst the Branches

Birds tease each other with chirpy wit,
Flapping about, they never sit.
"Tweet the day away!" one does proclaim,
While others join in the punny game.

Rustling leaves hold a joke or two,
Creating laughter as breezes blew.
In the thicket, faces bloom,
As humor chases away the gloom.

Jest in the Jewel-toned Jungle

In a jungle bright with color and fun,
Vines twist together, a playful run.
Parrots squawk with comedic flair,
As monkeys joke and swing in the air.

Lizards lounge with their smirky grins,
While tigers chuckle, sharing their sins.
All around, nature laughs in delight,
In this wild world, everything feels right.

Humorous Hues in the Hemlock

In the shade where squirrels debate,
A raccoon claims he's truly great.
With acorns tossed as prizes rare,
The trees just shake, without a care.

A chipmunk dons a tiny hat,
And dances round a slumbering cat.
While shadows laugh, the sun just beams,
The forest cracks with giggly dreams.

A toad croaks jokes; a tree frog sighs,
Their punchlines leap through leafy highs.
Each bough and branch, a friend to tease,
As nature's jesters frolic with ease.

So gather 'round, where laughter grows,
In hidden nooks, where humor flows.
Among the trunks, a cheer unfolds,
With every tale the woodland holds.

Lively Legends from the Leafy Depths

The owl hoots tales of silly fights,
Where fireflies twinkle like little lights.
A hedgehog plays a game of tags,
And raccoons dance with bags and rags.

A fox in boots struts with delight,
Claiming he's the sultan of the night.
The nightingale sings songs of cheer,
While bushes giggle, "Hear! Hear!"

Each breeze tells tales of nuts and seeds,
As squirrels plot their daring deeds.
With acorns flying, laughter rings,
An orchestra of woodland things.

So stop a while, let laughter bloom,
In leafy nooks where joy finds room.
These lively tales, a sweet surprise,
In nature's heart, where humor lies.

Clever Capers in the Clouded Canopy

A parrot squawks with witty flair,
While monkeys swing without a care.
They trade wisecracks in airy leaps,
Among the clouds, where humor creeps.

The vines get tangled, giggles grow,
As butterflies put on a show.
They flit and flutter, tease the air,
With every twist, they dance with flair.

Beneath the leaves, a party starts,
With ladybugs and bouncing hearts.
A caterpillar cracks a jest,
As tree trunks stand, all dressed the best.

The whispers of the wind bring glee,
In shimmering light, a jubilee.
So join the fun, where laughter swings,
In clouded heights and playful things.

Giggles Among the Grounded Grasses

In meadows wide, where daisies sway,
A rabbit hops, "Just one more play!"
With every bounce, his tale unfolds,
Of mischief made, and laughter bold.

The crickets chirp a tune so sweet,
While ants march on with tiny feet.
They share their snacks, a feast of fun,
Beneath the rays of setting sun.

A butterfly, with colors bright,
Tells jokes to snails, a comical sight.
With whispered giggles in the breeze,
They bring to life the gentlest tease.

So stroll along through grassy dreams,
Where humor flows in sunny streams.
For nature's laughter fills the space,
In every nook, you'll find your place.

Wordplay in the Whispering Woods

In a forest where the puns reside,
Trees chuckle as they wave with pride.
Squirrels flicking tails, a cheeky sight,
Banter echoes, a true delight.

Mushrooms giggle in a dainty dance,
They trip on roots, but take a chance.
Foxes cracking jokes in clever ways,
While owls hoot in playful praise.

Breezes carry laughter through the air,
Every echo, a whimsical flair.
Nature's jesters, they never tire,
In this grove, where smiles aspire.

A raccoon snickers with a grin,
"Why did the chicken? Oh, do begin!"
Whispers swirl in this leafy haunt,
In the wildwood, humor's a font.

Clever Catchphrases of the Canopy

Beneath the limbs where jokes take flight,
Laughter bounces, morning to night.
A parrot squawks, "No prob... llama!"
While chipmunks break for nut-filled drama.

Branches sway with a sly, quick wit,
All the creatures know how to fit.
"Don't be stumped, it's all a game,"
Says the beetle, with a wink, not shame.

The sun dips low with a wink and nod,
Moths dress up for the evening plod.
"Buzz it up, don't let it slide!"
In the canopies, humor's our guide.

As shadows play, mischief unfurls,
Even the flowers wear silly pearls.
In this green realm where giggles reign,
Catchphrases bloom like summer rain.

Laugh Lines in the Luminescent Larks

In twilight's glow, the larks take flight,
Tickled by moonbeams, oh what a sight!
Songs that prance, with a ticklish sound,
 Bright notes shimmer, all around.

Crickets chirp in a rhythmic cheer,
"Knock, knock!" echoes, loud and clear.
Fireflies wink with a gleeful flash,
In tonight's show, they're a glowing bash.

Branches sway with a jocular hum,
Nature's band is a comical drum.
"Why so serious?" a crow tweets loud,
"Let's laugh it up, join the crowd!"

Each note spills forth like sparkling wine,
In the night air, where stars align.
Shimmers gleefully strut their stuff,
In this light-hearted realm, never enough.

Raucous Rhymes among the Redwoods

Amidst the giants, a rhyme takes form,
Where laughter swells, a rustic charm.
A badger jokes with a bushy tail,
"Let's have a laugh, let's tip the scale!"

Redwoods whisper secrets, sly and deep,
Their ancient wisdom makes us leap.
"Leaf me alone, I'm shedding tears!"
Yet every bark brings out the cheers.

A raccoon strolls with a top hat askew,
"Counting stars? I've lost my cue!"
With each tall tale, the night rolls on,
Quips and gags until the dawn.

So gather close, where the shadows play,
In this scenic grove, we'll laugh all day.
Raucous rhymes under moonlit beams,
In the redwoods, we weave our dreams.

Lighthearted Lore of the Lilacs

In the garden, frogs debate,
Who can jump to a better fate.
With crowns of petals oh so bright,
They croak and chuckle through the night.

Bumblebees buzz with fancy flair,
Telling tales of flowers fair.
They sip the nectar, make it sweet,
While dancing 'round on little feet.

A squirrel jesters with a nut,
Claiming he's the greatest shut.
With acorn caps as hats he wears,
He jokes about his furry flares.

The lilacs sway, a jest they tell,
Of pollinators and their spell.
In laughter, blooms and bees unite,
Creating joy from morn to night.

The Sassy Symphony of the Sycamores

Sycamores shake with sass so grand,
Their branches dance, a cheeky band.
With swaying limbs, they tease the breeze,
Inviting whispers through the leaves.

A woodpecker drums a silly beat,
While squirrels engage in a swift retreat.
Beneath the branches, critters meet,
In harmony, they find their seat.

A grumpy owl offers a wise remark,
As rabbits hop, and the shadows spark.
Chirping songs of little delight,
The forest hums well into the night.

With every rustle, laughter flows,
A lively rhythm that grows and grows.
In sycamore's embrace, we discover,
The joy of nature, like no other.

Laughs Beneath the Leafy Lattice

Beneath a canopy so bright,
The chatter lingers with pure delight.
A raccoon, masked with a clever grin,
Claims he's the king; let the games begin!

With shadows dancing, tales unfold,
Of secrets whispered, both brave and bold.
A chipmunk sneaks, all full of cheer,
Filling his cheeks, a nervous leer.

The breeze carries whispers, tricks galore,
As creatures gather, seeking out more.
In a tangle of vines, the laughter weaves,
Creating joy that never leaves.

Each leaf sways to the funny sound,
These silly moments, forever abound.
In nature's embrace, we find our way,
To humor that brightens every day.

Gags in the Glade of Green

In the glade where mischief thrives,
A turtle tells how he strives.
"Slow and steady, that's my game,
But watch me win, it's quite the claim!"

A hedgehog rolls, no sense of fear,
Spinning tales that bring good cheer.
With quills arranged like a fine bouquet,
He tosses jokes and rolls away.

The trees chuckle, their bark like guffaws,
As foxes tease with playful paws.
In the green, where laughter blooms,
Each sound lifts spirits and dispels glooms.

So gather round in nature's play,
In every nook, there's humor at bay.
In the glade where joy runs free,
The world's a stage for you and me.

Puns Lurking in the Petals

In the garden where jokes bloom bright,
A daffodil grins with all its might.
Petals whisper tales of glee,
"Lettuce laugh, come join me!"

Sweet peas chirp with cheery puns,
Chasing shadows, having fun.
Daisy's cry, a playful cheer,
"Stop and smell the laughs right here!"

Sapling Shenanigans

Tiny trunks with grin so wide,
Beneath the sun, they toss aside.
Twisting branches, a crooked dance,
Saplings giggle with every chance.

Roots interlace like friends in tune,
Chasing critters 'neath the moon.
They whisper jokes in rustling leaves,
"Hey, who knew trees could be such thieves?"

Surreal Smiles Under the Wild Vines

Beneath the vines where laughter creeps,
A chortling breeze through foliage sweeps.
Twisted tendrils tickle the air,
"Is that a joke? Oh, do I dare!"

Raspberry bushes roll their eyes,
With every twist, a new surprise.
"Why did the grape stop to chat?
Because it found a friend—how about that?"

The Lighthearted Legacies of Lush Landscapes

In the wilds where giggles grow,
The landscape's tales begin to flow.
Bouncing boulders and jolly streams,
Crafting laughter from wild dreams.

Meadows dance with sunshine's glee,
As daisies share their history.
Frolicsome fables, far and wide,
Nature's show, a joyful ride.

Pithy Phrases of the Pine Path

In the forest of chatter, squirrels debate,
What's better than nuts? Oh, just wait!
A turtle in sunglasses strides with great flair,
Claiming it's speed, though we know it's a dare.

A raccoon with a mask steals a grand feast,
Saying, "I'm just here for the best of the least!"
While owls hoot jokes that deeply annoy,
The hedgehogs snicker, oh what a ploy!

The tall trees listen, with branches that sway,
To gossip of snails and their slow-motion play.
Frogs crack their jokes; the drakes try to quack,
While fireflies flicker, adding spark to the pack.

With laughter that echoes, the woodland's alive,
From moss-covered rocks, quirky thoughts will derive.
Each creature contributes to this merry sound,
In the pines where humor and nature are found.

Nonsense in the Nestled Nooks

In a nook where the breezes whistled a tune,
A chameleon's quip made a balloon swoon.
"Why change your color when you can change mood?"
Belly-laughing lizards embrace the absurd food.

A fox with a bowtie addressed the whole crowd,
Said, "I'll be fancy but never too loud!"
With each little chuckle that speckled the air,
A snake told a tale that sparked quite a scare.

Bumblebees buzzed with a clear sense of rhyme,
Claiming that honey was worth every dime.
The hedgehog retorted, "That's quite a tall tale!
What's wealth without friends? It's destined to fail!"

And so in the corners, where laughter abounds,
Nature's quirks echo, in delightful surrounds.
In this playful realm, nonsense reigns true,
As creatures of whimsy stumble anew.

Sarcasm Spun from Silhouetted Shrubs

In shadows of shrubs where the wit never sleeps,
A deer quips, "Oh look, it's my favorite creeps!"
With a flick of his ears and a nose in the air,
He whispers of foxes who think they're quite rare.

A badger joins in with a sarcastic wink,
Said, "Do you think they have time to rethink?"
As mice roll their eyes and toss crumbs in the breeze,
"Please give them a mirror; let's watch while they tease!"

The trees all nod slowly, their branches in jest,
While birds on the wires are clearly the best.
With each flapping joke, a new laugh is spun,
As humor takes flight in the soft morning sun.

Through the cracks and the creaks of the rustling leaves,
Each chuckle and chortle the woodland receives.
For in this green haven, where shadows still play,
Sarcasm is king, come join in the fray!

The Glee of Verdant Verses

Beneath canopies lush, the giggles resound,
As frogs craft limericks, humor unbound.
The flowers exchange tales, both silly and bright,
While shadows of bunnies delight in their plight.

A fox with a fable, oh what a charmer!
Spins yarns of lost berries that turned into armor.
While peacocks parade with their feathers on show,
Claiming they've got a great tale to throw.

The brook babbles softly, with puns on the flow,
As otters flip fish, in synchrony's show.
Each ripple a giggle, each splash a hoot,
Nature rejoices, in its lively pursuit.

In this glade full of glee, the verses entwine,
With laughter as lush as the green of the vine.
As dusk brings the stars, and the moon starts to gleam,
The joy of these woods fuels the heart like a dream.

Quips from the Canopy

A squirrel danced with such delight,
He wore a hat that sparkled bright.
The birds chimed in with cackling glee,
As branches shook with joy, set free.

A rabbit sneezed, oh what a sound!
It bounced so high, it touched the ground.
The flowers laughed with petals wide,
While butterflies turned side to side.

The fox, in hiding, cracked a joke,
But tripped on roots and nearly choked.
His laugh echoed through the green,
A sound so sweet, it must be seen.

A wise old owl, with good intent,
Said, "Whooo's the best? I say it's me!"
The laughter rippled through the trees,
As nature joined in joyous tease.

Laughter Lurks in the Leaves

In shadows deep, a prankster plays,
A hidden beetle with tricky ways.
He rolls a log, makes friends with bugs,
And cooks up fun in tiny mugs.

The mice throw parties, cheese all around,
While crickets chirp a lively sound.
They waltz and twirl beneath the moon,
A dance where everyone joins in soon.

A raccoon grins with a clever plan,
To steal a snack from the picnic clan.
But laughter rings—he's caught in the act,
His little heist is now a good fact.

Beneath the trees where whispers play,
The giggles bounce from night to day.
In leafy laughter, joy takes flight,
With every chuckle, the woods feel right.

Humorous Hoots and Howls

An owl flew past with a wink and nod,
"Who's there?" it asked, and then it plod.
A coyote howled in a silly tune,
The forest swayed like a rocking moon.

The porcupine quipped, "I'm prickly fun!
I'll tickle you pink till the day is done."
Weights of laughter sat heavy in air,
And critters chuckled without a care.

A skunk made a face, "Did you smell that?"
"Oh please, that's nonsense!" said a wary cat.
They burst into giggles at the thought so vile,
As scents of the forest met laughter with style.

With each friendly jest, the night wore on,
In hoots and howls, all worries gone.
An echo of glee rang out through the trees,
For humor's embrace brought joyous ease.

The Forest's Playful Prose

In the heart of green, tales intertwine,
A fox chose words, so fancifully fine.
"I can outsmart," he said with flair,
"Just don't ask me to share my lair!"

A hedgehog chimed in, soft-spoken, wise,
"Life's about laughter, not just the prize."
They gathered around, tales spun with grace,
Under the moon's smile, a glowing embrace.

The frogs croaked verses, both silly and bright,
"Leap and laugh, it's a perfect night!"
The trees did sway in a rhythmic dance,
Each rhyme a beat in the forest's romance.

So let's toast a glass to this leafy stage,
Where every critter writes a funny page.
With nature as scribe, the stories unfold,
A tapestry woven with laughter bold.

Forest Riddles and Raucous Laughter

In shadows deep where secrets dwell,
The trees conspire, they weave and tell.
A squirrel jokes, oh what a show,
He flips a nut, the crowd says whoa!

A rustle here, a chirp in glee,
The owl hoots jokes with wild decree.
A bear wants in, but he's too slow,
He trips on roots, oh dear, oh no!

The rabbit cracks a pun on thorns,
While foxes roll in leafy adorns.
"Why did the twig refuse to bend?"
"Because it had a knotty friend!"

Amidst the green, the laughter streams,
While sunlight dances, the forest beams.
In every corner, humor finds,
A cheeky joke that nature binds.

Jests Beneath the Canopy

A chattering parrot, so spry and bright,
Tells tales of mischief from morning to night.
"Why was the tree so good at math?"
"Because it knew its roots and path!"

The bushes giggle as thorns poke fun,
While the deer prance, a frolicsome run.
A crow caws loud with a quip so keen,
"Life's a joke, but I'm the queen!"

The breeze makes faces as it sweeps by,
Tickling the leaves, oh my, oh my!
"Knock knock!" yells a chipmunk, quick as a flash,
"Who's there?" cries the toad, in a gleeful clash.

With each rustling laugh, the woods unite,
Creating a symphony, pure delight.
In nature's embrace, the bonds grow tight,
As laughter echoes into the night.

The Playful Palette of the Pines

A painter sits beneath the green,
With brushes made of whiskers, seen.
"Why paint a wall when you can draw?"
"Nature's a canvas, with rules to thaw!"

The pines sway gently, wearing a grin,
Taunting the creatures that pass them in.
"Why do squirrels hide their supply?"
"Because they're nutty, oh my, oh my!"

Fish in the brook frolic with pride,
Swapping tall tales of the current tide.
"Catch of the day?" one fish did joke,
"It's all in the gills, don't choke on smoke!"

As colors splash in this woodland scene,
Every shadow dances, vibrant and keen.
In this playful haven, jokes are our lore,
A tapestry woven that we all adore.

Banter Beneath the Branches

Beneath the branches, jokes bloom bright,
As nimble creatures frolic in flight.
"Why did the acorn roll away?"
"Because it wanted to play all day!"

The wind whispered secrets to buds on high,
While birds exchanged puns that made them sigh.
"A hawk just laughed, can you believe?
He's winging it, but still conceives!"

The flowers giggled, each petal a word,
In this chorus, every pun heard.
"Why do bees always buzz along?"
"Because they know the sweet is where they belong!"

At dusk, the tales take flight in the air,
With every jest shared, dispelled every care.
The forest relishes in playful delight,
As laughter flows freely, a pure, shining light.

Winks of Wit in the Weeping Woods

Amid the trees where shadows leap,
The squirrels plot while rabbits creep.
A crow tells jokes with a clever caw,
While mushrooms giggle—what a law!

The brook babbles secrets in playful guise,
And crickets chirp with knowing sighs.
In every nook, a laugh to find,
Nature's punchlines, sweetly entwined.

Breezes whisper as they tease,
Tickling leaves with playful ease.
Foxes frolic, tails a-flare,
Comedic moments fill the air.

When the sun dips low and shadows grow,
The wildwood hums with a vibrant glow.
A cacophony of chuckles blend,
In this funny realm, the joy won't end.

The Chuckles of the Charmed Canopy

Up above, the branches sway,
With laughter floating on the way.
The owls wink with wisdom bright,
While squirrels dance, what a sight!

Dandelions toss their heads around,
As ants parade in a merry sound.
Each blade of grass holds a jest,
In this canopy, you're truly blessed.

Frogs croak jokes as they leap,
While ladybugs their secrets keep.
The moon beams down, a playful smile,
Lighting up the woods for a while.

So join the fun, let laughter ring,
Let every twig and critter sing.
In this enchanted, charming place,
A chuckle thrives in nature's embrace.

Mimicry of the Merriment Mott

In the mott where mischief brews,
Little creatures know the cues.
A bear pretends to dance on toes,
While a fox in caper slyly goes.

Bats hang low in a comic pose,
While rabbits wear their best clothes.
There's humor found in each small space,
As creatures join the merry race.

The wind plays tricks with a tinkling laugh,
Tickling ferns, it's quite the gaffe.
Even the stones crack a grin,
As laughter bubbles from within.

So stroll through this jolly little dell,
Where every shrub has a tale to tell.
Find joy in nature's amusing plot,
In the heart of the mott, we laugh a lot.

Tales Told by the Thicket Pals

Beneath the thicket, tales unfold,
Of critters brave and spirits bold.
With a raccoon wearing a funny hat,
And a bear who swears he's part acrobat.

Chirping birds make a choir sound,
While hedgehogs twirl upon the ground.
Each leaf is ripe with a story shared,
Of friendship here, nothing compared.

A playful breeze whispers and spins,
Encouraging giggles, where joy begins.
Every critter, in laughter's thrall,
Tells a tale to enthrall us all.

So gather 'round, let your worries cease,
In this thicket, find your peace.
With pals so clever, you'll surely see,
Life's funnier side, wild and free.

Epigrams in the Emerald Empyrean

In the forest bright, where squirrels dance,
A chipmunk cracks a nutty romance.
With acorn hats and laughter loud,
They jest in shadows, a merry crowd.

The owl winks twice, a sage in disguise,
With riddles wrapped in moonlit skies.
Beneath tall trees, the banter flies,
As crickets chirp their comic sighs.

A rabbit thinks he's quite the chap,
In sneakers made from a soft cotton flap.
He shares tall tales of his nightly laps,
While foxes chuckle in quiet claps.

Together they weave a jolly scene,
In emerald halls where laughter's seen.
A merry band of nature's lore,
In the treetops, forevermore.

Sprightly Sentences of the Spruce

Beneath the spruces, mischief brews,
As raccoons share their midnight views.
With masks of bandits, they plot and scheme,
In their eyes, a twinkle—a playful dream.

A parrot squawks a verse so bright,
"Why did the branch fall? It lost its fight!"
The laughter echoes through the glade,
With every joke, the tension fades.

A porcupine boasts of his cool spikes,
"I'm a walking fortress—no need for hikes!"
While woodpeckers drum their rhythmic cheer,
Together they spread the joy sincere.

In this wonderland where humor flows,
Each critter knows how laughter grows.
Sprightly sentences, quick and spry,
In the spruce-filled night, they soar and fly.

Parables from the Periphery

Among the edges where shadows mingle,
A frog croaks tales with a funny jingle.
He chats with flies about his great leap,
While toads in tune, a chorus keep.

A butterfly flirts in colorful flair,
"Ever tried to catch me? Oh, what a dare!"
With wings like whispers, they dance and tease,
Among the blossoms, they float with ease.

A hedgehog grins, his quills all a-spike,
Says, "I'm simply poking fun—what's the like?"
His laughter bristles through the moor,
Spreading joy like sunlight on the forest floor.

In this periphery, humor thrives,
Where every rascal knows how to drive
The spirit of jest, in tales combined,
Leaving a trail of giggles behind.

Lively Lines in the Lushness

In the lush embrace where nature plays,
Lively lines dance through sunny rays.
With bouncing bunnies, and seals in hats,
Every creature sports their silliest spats.

A bear hums songs about honeyed treats,
While dancing deer tap their dainty feet.
The laughter echoes through leafy trails,
As frogs compose their ribbiting tales.

A chorus of crickets serenely cry,
"Why don't trees play cards? They're always shy!"
With punchlines tucked in every nook,
Nature's comedy fills the brook.

Within the vivid, verdant scene,
Each chuckle's bright, each smile a sheen.
In lively lines, the wild twirls,
And nature's laughter eternally unfurls.

Jocular Journeys through Hidden Glades

In the glade where laughter spills,
A fox dons spectacles and takes his thrills.
Squirrels join a comical race,
With acorns flying all over the place.

Beneath the bark, a wise old tree,
Tells jokes so bad, you'll want to flee.
But listen close, you might just find,
Giggles tucked within the pine.

Wandering paths where echoes sing,
A bench made of mushrooms? What a thing!
Join the dance of the giggling fey,
Who turn the mundane into a play.

So pack your chuckles, come take a stroll,
In this woodland realm where humor is the goal.
Each step a jest, each glance a grin,
In these hidden glades, the joy begins.

Charms and Chortles of the Cedar

Amongst the cedars, laughter flows,
A raccoon with a hat, who knows how it goes.
Twisting tales of mischief and mirth,
Turn every corner into a burst of worth.

The birds all chirp in a cheeky tune,
As the sun peeks out in the afternoon.
A squirrel shares gossip that makes you snicker,
About the owl who tried to be a flicker.

With roots that chuckle and branches sway,
The secrets of joy guide the way.
Gather 'round as the stories unfold,
In the heart of the cedar, where fun's pure gold.

So let the laughter in the air spread,
Creating smiles, no reason to dread.
In the charming shade of the cedar tree,
Find comic gems, just wait and see.

The Humor Hidden in the Henge

In the henge where shadows play,
A stone-cold statue shimmies away.
It winks and giggles, what a sight,
Making all the fairies take flight.

Crowns of daisies on heads of bees,
Buzzing jokes carried on the breeze.
A rabbit recites a stand-up show,
With punchlines that steal the evening glow.

At dusk, a lantern glows with glee,
Reading laughter left like notes on a tree.
Each pebble whispers a joke or two,
While the moon chuckles; you join in too.

So gather round with friends in hand,
In the henge where giggles expand.
With ancient stones and spirits around,
The humor here is happily found.

Bright Banter Among the Blossoms

In the garden where colors clash,
Bees buzz gossip, and blossoms flash.
A dandy deer struts with flair,
While roses share tales beyond compare.

Flirting with daisies, a bumblebee,
Whispers sweetly, "Come dance with me!"
Petals giggling in soft sunlight,
Paint a picture of pure delight.

Banter flows like a gentle stream,
As nature plays out its morning dream.
Each flower's quip, a blossom's jest,
In this vibrant patch, we feel blessed.

So stroll through this canvas, bright and gay,
Where laughter and blooms light the way.
In the heart of the petals, take your seat,
And let the humor make your day sweet.

Leaps of Wit in Leafy Lanes

Squirrel in shades, doing a dance,
Mice chuckle softly, given a chance.
Frogs in a chorus, croaking in rhyme,
Tickled by leaves, it's humor time!

Butterflies giggle in sunlight's embrace,
Nectar-filled laughter fills up the place.
With every rustle, a joke on the air,
The woods are alive with humor to share!

Rabbits swap tales, their ears standing tall,
A jest about carrots leaves everyone small.
Laughter erupts as the sun sets low,
In leafy lanes where fun tends to grow!

So come take a stroll in this jokesome glade,
Where every small creature has laughter displayed.
Among the tall trees, this humor still reigns,
With leaps of pure wit down the leafy lanes.

Riddles in the Roots

Beneath the old oak, where shadows convene,
A fox spins a riddle, clever and keen.
"Why did the mushroom get invited to play?"
"Because he's a fun guy—what more can I say?"

The tortoise chuckles, slow but quite bright,
"Here's my riddle, for a giggle tonight.
What runs but never walks, has a bed but won't sleep?"
With laughter around, the answer's a creek!

The roots twist and turn, holding secrets in chat,
The ants keep a secret, finding that flat.
"Why do we gather? What's all of this fuss?"
"Because we're just tiny, but together, we're us!"

In the depths of the wood, where riddles delight,
The roots share their whispers, oh what a sight!
So gather your thoughts, and let laughter sprout,
With riddles and roots, it's what life's about!

Chortles of the Chatty Chipmunks

Chipmunks in bushes, fluffing their cheeks,
Gossip and giggles, the chatter peaks.
"Did you hear, dear friend, about the lost acorn?"
"I heard it rolled off, from dusk until dawn!"

In twirls and somersaults, they play and react,
Jokes that bounce back, no need to retract.
One hints of berries, another cracks wise,
With laughter resounding, brightening skies!

Racing through ferns, they mock race with glee,
"Last one to lunch, please stay by the tree!"
Chortles erupt as they dart to and fro,
The antics of chipmunks—a humorous show!

So join in the fun, this woodland parade,
With chatty chipmunks, where smiles never fade.
Life's little pleasures, in jests and in games,
Bringing joy in the wildwood—with no one to blame!

Jestful Journeys through the Green

On a trail through the green where the wild things sing,
Squirrels and badgers, what laughter they bring!
"Why did the tree go to school for a while?"
"Because it wanted to improve its branch style!"

The whispering leaves join in with delight,
As hedgehogs parade in the soft morning light.
With each clever jest, and every quick quip,
A jestful journey, a fellowship trip!

Old owl on a branch, wise but still spry,
"Here's a riddle that will surely make you sigh.
What has feathers but never takes flight?"
"Why a quilt, of course, it's a cozy delight!"

In meadows so lush, where laughter feels free,
The tales spin around like a joyous decree.
As friends in the green share a whimsical thread,
Remember the laughter, and joy that they spread!

Playful Parables in the Pine Barrens

The squirrel donned a tiny hat,
Claiming he was the king of the spat.
He scolded the owl, with a pompous flair,
'You hoot too much, no one's aware!'

In shadows deep, the rabbits compare,
Who has the best carrots, if you dare.
They giggled and hopped, with tales to share,
Of garden raids and a fox's glare.

The raccoon, a thief, with mask so bold,
Stole a sandwich, or so the story's told.
He pranced on the path, tail flicking with glee,
'Catch me if you can!' was his sneaky decree.

Among the pines, laughter flows bright,
With each little creature, a spark of delight.
They weave their tales, from dawn till dusk,
In the heart of the woods, where joy is a must.

Jests that Danced on the Dew

A dragonfly spun, a belly full of cheer,
It twirled and whirled, no sign of fear.
"It's my birthday today!" it happily spun,
"Join in the dance, let's have some fun!"

Beneath the ferns, a toad found a throne,
Croaked out a joke, in a croaky tone.
The crickets laughed, while counting the beats,
"Your kingdom's so small; is it just your feet?"

The mushrooms giggled, dressed in their caps,
Sharing their dreams, avoiding the mishaps.
"Let's grow a tall tale, out of the blue,
Of giants who stumble, and run from the dew!"

As morning sun brightened the wallowing glade,
Nature's own jesters, a light-hearted parade.
In the sparkle of dawn, on leaves all anew,
The laughter persists, like the morning dew.

Stories Sprouted from Sticks

A stick stood tall, with stories to tell,
Of Nibbler the mouse, and his cheese-loving spell.
'The bigger the bite, the sweeter the find!'
He shared with the flock, always so kind.

Branches swayed gently, whispering fame,
Of a snail who raced in a thrilling game.
'You'll never believe, I won by a shell!'
The beetles all chuckled, 'Oh do tell, do tell!'

The fox with a grin, tried to play on words,
Said, "All my best jokes are for the birds!"
They fluttered and flapped, joyous in flight,
In a skit of surprise, pure delight in the night.

Amidst the twigs, laughter unfolds,
In woodland's embrace, where mischief beholds.
For stories sprouted, as wild creatures weave,
The best kinds of tales are the ones we believe.

Whimsical Whispers in Wooded Hollows

In shadowy nooks, secrets are spoken,
A chipmunk chuckled, 'My acorn's a token!`
'Want to trade it for nuts or a sweet berry pie?'
The laughter erupted, under the sky.

A jolly old bear took his time on a quest,
To find the best honey and see who's the best.
With each sticky paw, he left trail of goo,
'Follow my path for a sticky sweet view!'

A sly little lizard, with a wink and a grin,
Said, "I'm more than a reptile, I'm a magician!"
He vanished in leaves, then popped out with flair,
"Did you see that? I can disappear in thin air!"

In these wooded halls, joy's never far,
With tales of enchantment, like bright shooting stars.
So gather 'round, friends, let's share in the cheer,
For whimsy is wild when nature draws near.

Jests of the Wistful Willow

In the shade where willows sway,
A squirrel tells jokes at break of day.
The breeze carries laughter through the leaves,
As creatures chuckle, no one deceives.

A rabbit hops in, ears flopping wide,
He shares his puns with a hop and glide.
With every whisper, the shadows grin,
While the old tree chuckles, letting joy in.

Behind the trunk, a fox rolls on grass,
"Why did the chicken cross?" he lets it pass.
The answer is lost, but spirits so high,
Make every dull moment seem to fly.

As twilight approaches, the joy won't cease,
The willow grins softly, a picture of peace.
For in this wild place, humor thrives,
Where laughter's the currency, and fun survives.

Mirth in the Misty Glen

Through the mist where giggles bloom,
Frogs croak tales in a tiny room.
The crickets chirp, a chorus so bright,
In the glen of mirth, laughter takes flight.

A hedgehog pipes up, with a prickly cheer,
"Why do we wear this armor, dear?
To win against foes who simply admire,
It keeps us safe, we won't retire!"

Chasing fireflies, the night so sweet,
Each glow a joke, a rhythmic beat.
A dance of shadows, folly on show,
As moonlit giggles dance to and fro.

With every twinkle in the night sky,
Creatures unite in a joyful sigh.
For in this enchanting, misty embrace,
Laughter and love find their favored place.

Antics of the Adventurous Alder

An alder stands tall, with limbs stretched wide,
Sharing secrets and laughter, a source of pride.
A bluebird sings songs with a cheeky tone,
While squirrels exchange winks from their throne.

A badger strolls in, a confident fella,
"Knock, knock," he begins, "Who's the best fella?"
"It's me, dear friends, here to make you smile,
Watch my antics, stay for a while!"

The pond reflects all the playful scene,
Where frogs leap high, wearing crowns of green.
"Why sit and ponder when we can play?
Life is a jest, let's laugh the day away!"

In the warmth of the sun, the glee cascades,
Alder rejoices, its humor invades.
Boundless and bright, in nature's own rhyme,
These antics of joy, refreshing as time.

A Symphony of Snickers among the Shrubs

Among the shrubs where giggles grow,
A rabbit and turtle exchange a show.
"Why did you hide?" chirps the bold thrush,
"In the thicket of weeds, you're quick in a rush!"

"Because," squeaks the turtle, with a thoughtful blink,
"When things get tough, I find time to think!"
But the rabbit just chuckles, already aware,
A shrub's whispering secrets beyond compare.

As owls hoot softly, wise yet sly,
They share tales of jest, oh how they'd fly!
Every branch and leaf joins in the cheer,
Together they liven the atmosphere here.

So if you wander through this lush maze,
Listen close for those joking phrases.
In this leafy world, let your heart sway,
For a symphony of snickers brightens the day.

Mirth in the Misty Maize

In a field where corn does sway,
The scarecrow cracks jokes every day.
He says, 'Why don't you ever crawl?
Because you might trip on a kernel ball!'

The crows congregate, not in fright,
They cackle loud, what a sight!
One shouts, 'We've got a grand design,
To steal his hat, oh, it'll be fine!'

Amidst the stalks, laughter swirls,
Nature's jest holds secret pearls.
'Why do corn stalks stand so tall?
Because they're afraid of the kernel fall!'

With each giggle, the sun shines bright,
Even the shadows dance in delight.
Here in the maze, joy is the trend,
Let mirth and maize be the perfect blend.

Folly under the Foliage

Under leaves where whispers play,
Frogs play cards at the end of the day.
One croaks, 'I'm all in, what do you say?
Don't ribbit out now, it's a game of sway!'

The rabbit hops by with a grin,
Says, 'You'll never win; it's my kin!'
'Oh, don't be hasty,' the snail declares,
'I've seen frogs miss, and it leaves them in airs!'

A squirrel chimes in with a laugh,
'You lumpy toads can't even do math!'
Amid branches and twigs, friendly jests,
Claim joy in this folly that never rests.

As dusk descends with a twinkling star,
The critters recount tales from afar.
Beneath the foliage, hearts feel the glee,
In folly's embrace, they are truly free.

Whispers Amidst the Woods

Deep in the woods where shadows frolic,
The trees gossip, always symbolic.
One says, 'Did you hear the owl's tease?
He hoots like a rock star, aiming to please!'

The brook bubbles with a giggling sound,
While squirrels scamper, round and round.
They whisper tales of acorns lost,
'That treasure chest? What a hefty cost!'

A deer prances with a smirk so sly,
'Why did the chicken cross? Oh, why oh why?'
Lost in laughter, they leap and twine,
Nature's humor is perfectly divine.

Under the moon, with laughter unbound,
Even the shadows join in the sound.
In whispers of joy, the forest finds light,
Filling the night with pure delight.

Clever Conversations Under Canopy

Beneath the branches where chatter rings,
Bees debate the best of flings.
One buzzes, 'I'm sweet, let's compare!
But who has the finest floral flair?'

A rabbit hops close, ears all perked,
Chimes in quick, 'Your floral work's lurked!
I'm the fastest, you just can't see,
How I outrun you, buzzing with glee!'

The leafy greens with humor unfold,
Whispering secrets, both new and old.
A wise old tree shakes its bark and says,
'Let's celebrate life in silly ways!'

With giggles that float like drifting pollen,
The canopy hums, and spirits are callin'.
In clever repartee, all the critters play,
In this vibrant world, joy leads the way.

Sassy Shadows in the Sundrenched Grove

In the grove where sunlight plays,
Shadows dance in silly ways,
A squirrel grins with acorn flair,
Telling jokes without a care.

Laughter bounces on the breeze,
Trees join in with rustling leaves,
A rabbit hops, a jester bold,
Spouting tales both new and old.

Beneath the boughs of dappled light,
The critters frolic, hearts so bright,
A fox adds spice with clever quips,
As sunlight drips from leafy tips.

Here in this grove, the fun won't cease,
With every twirl, a bit of peace,
Sassy shadows, fun's embrace,
A world of joy in nature's space.

Chatter of the Chipmunks

In the thicket, chatter springs,
Chipmunks boast of little things,
A pinecone prize, a seedling score,
Their giggles echo, never a bore.

One claims to be the fastest sprinter,
While others argue, hearts grow dimmer,
A riddle tossed among the bunch,
Leaves them puzzled, lost in a hunch.

With twinkling eyes and twitching tails,
They share their tales of daring trails,
Jumping high from branch to stump,
With every laugh, they gain a thump.

In the laughter, friendship blooms,
Beyond the dark, where sunshine looms,
Chatter loud, a playful night,
These chipmunks dance in sheer delight.

Lighthearted Legends of Leafy Lanes

In leafy lanes, where whispers fly,
Legends of yore seem to sigh,
A turtle boasts of ancient speed,
While frogs croak tales that allude to greed.

A wandering hare spins yarns so grand,
Of midnight runs across the sand,
With every hop, the stories grow,
In the light of dusk's warm glow.

The wise old owl, perched on high,
Nods along with a twinkling eye,
He adds his wisdom, laid-back, uncouth,
Turning fables into a light-hearted truth.

Among branches where laughter wins,
The leafy lanes tell tales akin,
With every twist, a playful wink,
In their world, all creatures think.

Lively Lyricism in Leafy Arbors

Under arbors green and wide,
The breezes hum, and critters glide,
A mouse recites with passion bright,
Whimsical verses in the twilight.

With each word, the branches sway,
A crow chirps in a sassy way,
A dance of rhyme beneath the stars,
Every line strums fancy guitars.

The hedgehog jests in gentle tones,
While dancing ants tap on their bones,
Their lively lyrics fill the air,
In every nook, a joyful flair.

The night unfolds with tones so sweet,
In leafy arbors, friends will meet,
Together they craft joy anew,
In every line, a laugh breaks through.

Intriguing Improv in the Ivy

Beneath the leaves where whispers play,
A squirrel juggles nuts all day.
With a twist of fate, he drops his prize,
A giggle erupts as it rolls by.

The rabbits dance in silly shoes,
While hedgehogs debate the latest news.
A vine swings low with a cheeky grin,
Nature's stage, let the antics begin!

A butterfly steals the spotlight bright,
While frogs croak tunes deep into the night.
Each twist and turn, they improvise,
In this leafy realm of laugh-filled skies.

With every rustle, a story unfolds,
Of wise old owls and tricks they hold.
In the ivy's heart, let the mischief grow,
As creatures unite in a humorous show.

Silly Soliloquies by the Stream

By the brook where bubbles sing,
A frog recites his royal fling.
With speckled skin and a dapper bow,
He leaps for laughs, take a front-row show!

A fish with dreams of being a star,
Complains the stream just won't take him far.
While ducks quack jokes about their nests,
And otters perform their water ballet tests.

A crab in a clip, declares it a crime,
To lose all the marbles from last year's rhyme.
With each splash and gleam, they share their plight,
In the twilight glow, everything feels right.

So gather 'round this watery stage,
Where giggles float and joys engage.
In this stream's embrace, the laughter flows,
Silly soliloquies in playful throes.

The Festive Folly of the Forest

In the woods where the wild things sway,
A bear dressed up for a Broadway play.
With honeyed notes and a comical strut,
He dances along with a beaver's nut.

While the trees applaud with rustling leaves,
And the moonlight shimmers like glittering thieves.
A party of pixies flits through the night,
Bopping to rhythms that feel so right.

A deer dons shades and spins around,
While the raccoons laugh at the sight they found.
With every step, the forest shakes,
A carnival of joy that never breaks.

So join the fun under starlit skies,
With giggles and grins, no need for goodbyes.
In this jubilant jive, let the world sway,
In the folly of the forest, let's play all day!

Raucous Revelry of the Rustic Round

Around the fire where the stories blaze,
A raccoon wears a hat from yesteryear's craze.
With a flick of his paw, he calls for a cheer,
As owls hoot tales most bizarre, oh dear!

The badger brings snacks, a feast so grand,
While the fox takes charge with a confident hand.
They share wild jokes that tickle the soul,
Underneath the moon's bright glowing coal.

With every laugh, the shadows dance,
And creatures join in a wacky prance.
From deer to rabbits, all gather near,
For a raucous revelry that draws them here.

So grab a seat by the campfire's glow,
In this rustic round, let the humor flow.
Through giggles and glee, the night's far from done,
As friendships are forged and laughter's the fun.

www.ingramcontent.com/pod-product-compliance
Lightning Source LLC
Chambersburg PA
CBHW072128070526
44585CB00016B/1577